New notes for 2nd finger

E flat B flat F natural C natural

dotted crotchet (dotted quarter-note)

semiquavers (sixteenths)

1. Start the show

Count 4 bars

Rock tempo

KB & DB

f

9

mf

13

f

17

mf cresc. *f*

21

mf

25

f

2. Banyan tree

C string special

Jamaican folk tune

2. Banyan tree – see page 30.

3. Heat haze

Relaxed KB & DB

mp

5 *cresc.* *mf*

9 *mp* *mf*

13 **pizz.**

To practise the main rhythm of this piece, try saying

'Hot and sun - ny.'

4. Medieval tale

Sadly KB & DB

mp legato

5 *mf* *mp*

9 *mf*

11 **rit.** *mp*

4. Medieval tale – see page 30.

5. *In memory* (for Eileen)

C string special

Count 2 bars

Gently

KB & DB

mp (*mf*) *espress.*

9

16

Slower

mp

5. *Cornish May song* – see page 30.

6. *Chase in the dark*

Count 2 bars

With menace

KB & DB

f

7

mp

11

mf

15

19

f

23

7. *Merrily danced the Quaker's wife*

Scottish folk tune

Jig

mf

5

f

9

13

7. *Merrily danced the Quaker's wife*
(ensemble part)

Scottish folk tune

Jig

mf

6

f

12

8. O leave your sheep

C string special

French folk tune

8. O leave your sheep – see page 31.

9. Jingle bells

10. Allegretto in C

Mozart

10. Allegretto in G – see page 31.

11. The Mallow fling

Irish folk tune

Count 2 bars

12. Noël

C string special

Daquin

12. Noël – see page 32.

13. Finale from the 'Water Music'

Handel

Moderato

f

5

mf

9

mp

13

17

f

p

21

(rall. 2nd time)

f

ff

13. Finale from the 'Water Music' – see page 32.

14. Ecossaise in G

(ensemble part)

Beethoven

15. Viola Time rag

Count 4 bars

KB & DB

16. Busy day

KB & DB

17. On the go!

Count 4 bars

KB & DB

18. Blue whale

C string special

KB & DB

18. *Yodelling song* – see page 33.

19. Takin' it easy

Count 4 bars

20. Mean street chase

C string special

20. Romani band—see page 33.

21. Ten thousand miles away

21. Ten thousand miles away
(lower part of violin duet)

22. *I got those viola blues*

KB & DB

Slow blues

mf

5

9

13

f

mf

17

f

mf

20

f

24

rall.

mp

f

This is the octave harmonic on the A string.

23. Air in C

23. *Air in G* – see page 34.

24. Prelude from 'Te Deum'

24. *Prelude from 'Te Deum'* – see page 34.

25. That's how it goes!

Luckily, this piece is not as hard as it looks!

New notes for 3rd finger

F sharp C sharp G sharp

26. Flamenco dance

(***FTR*** No. 28)

KB & DB

Olé!

f

7

mp

13

f

19

25

mp

31

pizz.

f

37

42

arco

f

47

cresc.

ff

27. Somebody's knocking at your door

(***FTR*** No. 30)

Spiritual

28. The old chariot

31. The old chariot
(ensemble part)

29. Adam in the garden

Jamaican folk tune

30. Air

Handel

32. *Air* – see page 35.

31. The wee cooper o' Fife

(***FTR*** No. 33; adapted melody)

Scottish folk tune

Gently

mp

mf

cresc.

Slower

32. Aerobics!

KB & DB

Fast!

f

1.

2.

Fine

mf

cresc.

D.C. al Fine

37. Aerobics! – see page 35.

33. *Caribbean sunshine*

(***FTR*** No. 38; ensemble part)

Calypso

KB & DB

mf

5

8

11

14

f

17

1.

mf

2.

ff

Ensemble parts

These additional parts are compatible with, and are numbered as, the pieces in *Fiddle Time Runners.*

2. Banyan tree

(lower part of violin duet)

Jamaican folk tune

4. Medieval tale

(ensemble part)

KB & DB

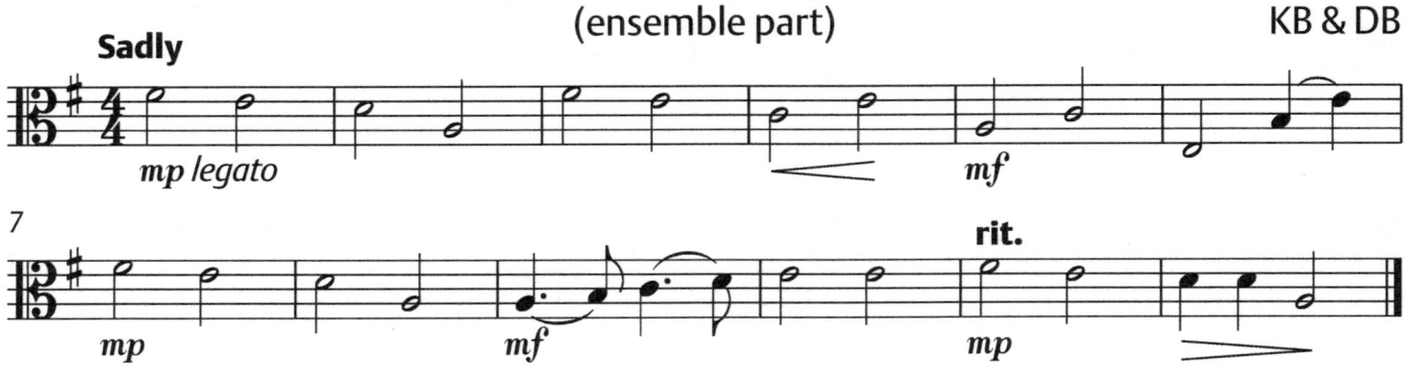

5. Cornish May song

(ensemble part)

Cornish folk tune

8. O leave your sheep

(lower part of violin duet)

French folk tune

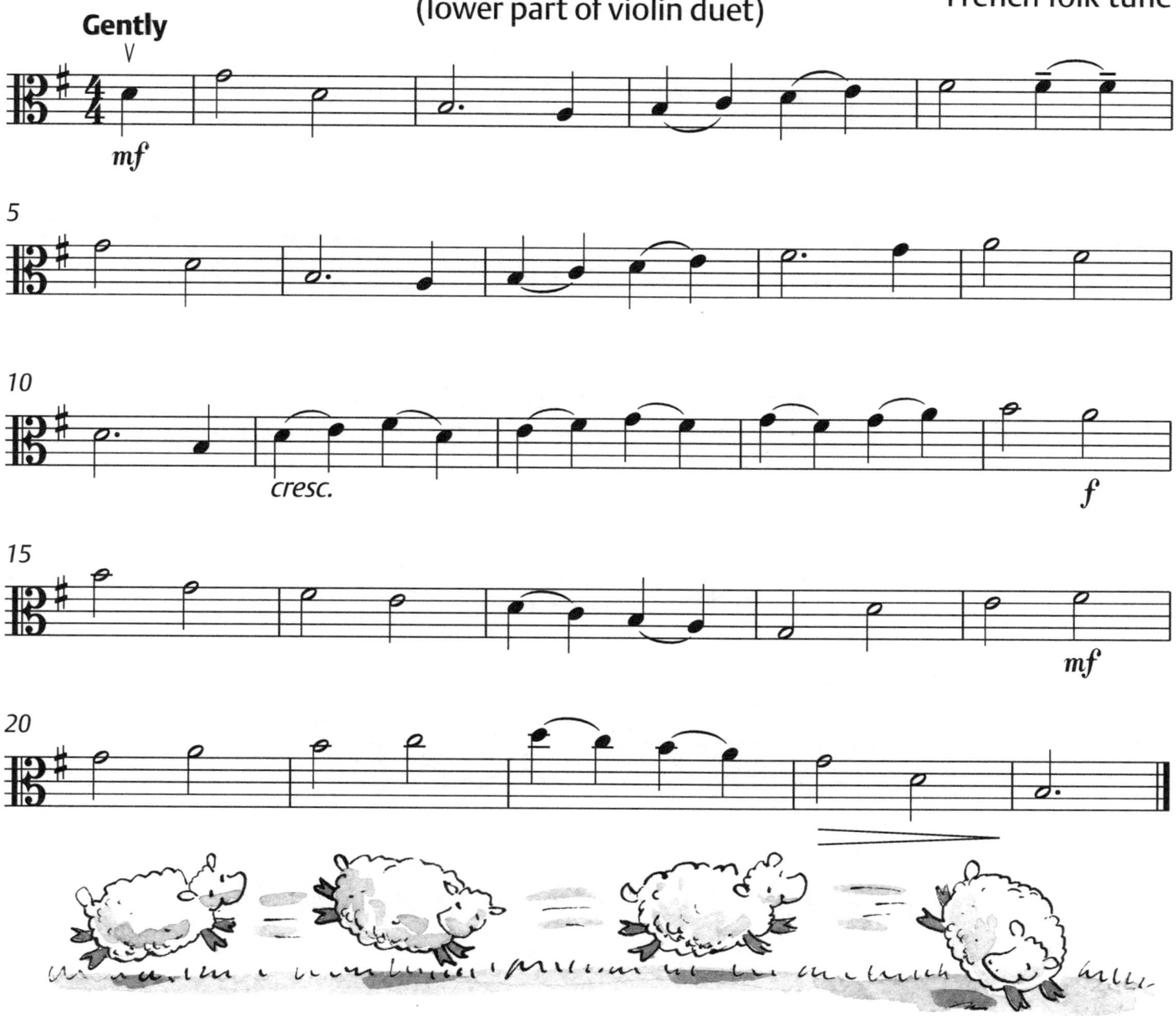

10. Allegretto in G

(ensemble part)

Mozart

12. Noël

(lower part of violin duet)

Daquin

Allegretto

13. Finale from the 'Water Music'

(ensemble part)

Handel

Moderato

18. Yodelling song

(melody)

German folk tune

20. Romani band

(melody)

KB & DB

23. Air in G

(ensemble part)

J. C. Bach

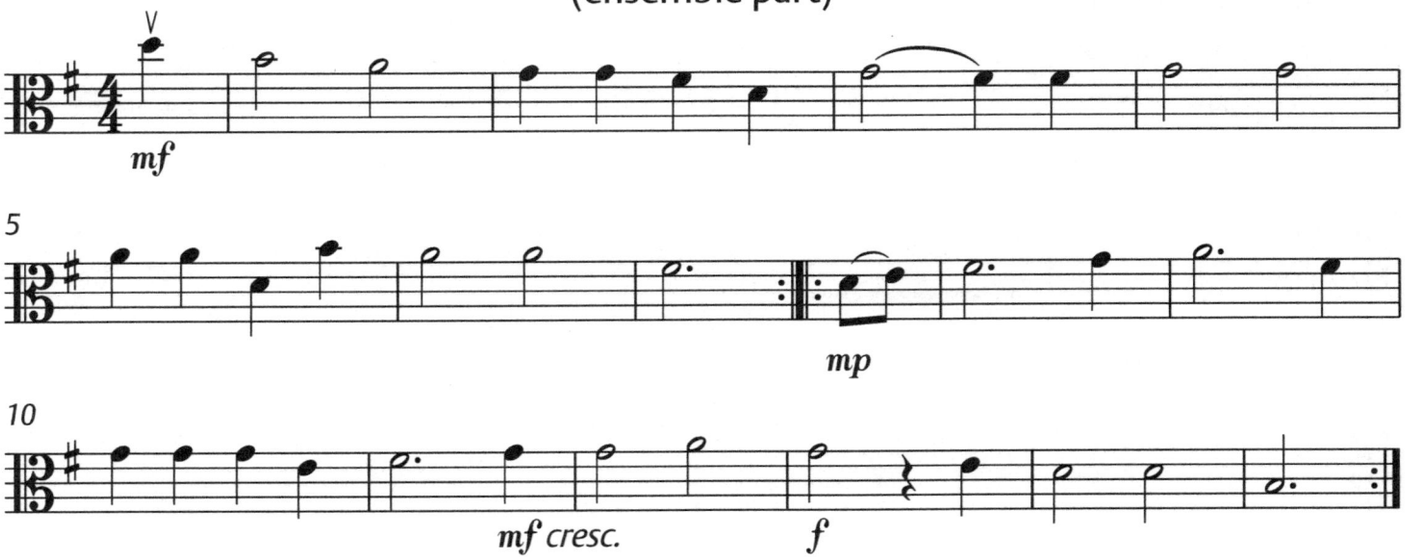

24. Prelude from 'Te Deum'

(ensemble part)

Charpentier

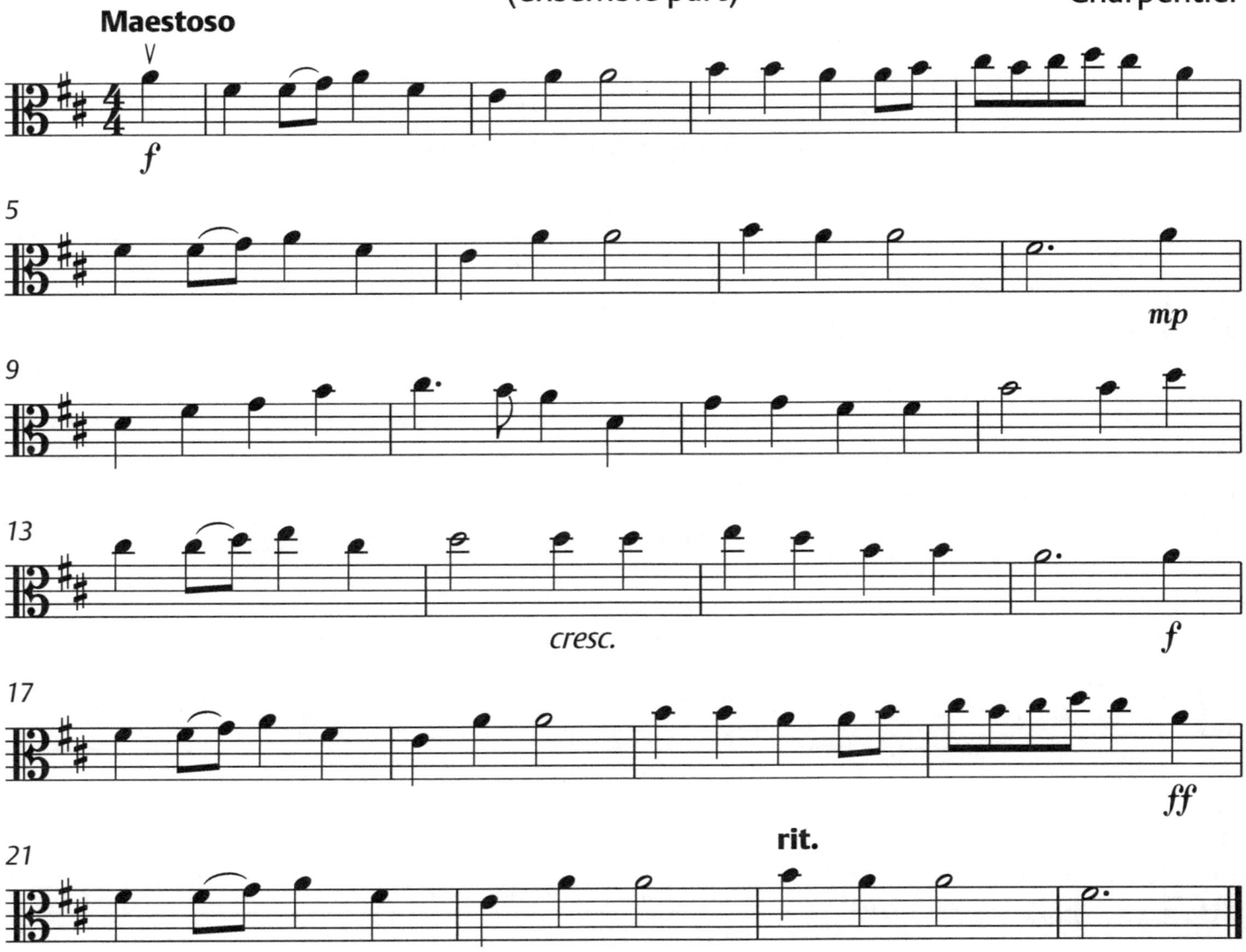

32. Air

(ensemble part for violin duet)

Handel

* Play these notes if the second violin part isn't played.

37. Aerobics!

(ensemble part)

KB & DB

Music Fact-Finder Page

Here are some of the words and signs you will find in some of your pieces!

How to play it

pizzicato or pizz. = pluck
arco = with the bow
⊓ = down bow
V = up bow
> = accent
𝅘𝅥𝅯𝄾 = tremolo

Don't get lost!

𝄆 𝄇 = repeat marks

1. 2. = first and second time bars
D.C. al Fine = repeat from the beginning and stop at **Fine**
D.𝄋 al Fine = repeat from the sign 𝄋 and stop at **Fine**
rit. or **rall.** = gradually getting slower
a tempo = back to the first speed
𝄐 = pause

Volume control

p (*piano*) = quiet
mp (*mezzo-piano*) = moderately quiet
mf (*mezzo-forte*) = moderately loud
f (*forte*) = loud
ff (*fortissimo*) = very loud
 or *crescendo* (*cresc.*) = getting gradually louder
 or *diminuendo* (*dim.*) = getting gradually quieter

Italian phrase-book

Allegro = fast and lively
Allegretto = not too fast
Andante = at a walking pace
legato = smoothly
Maestoso = majestically
Moderato = at a moderate speed
Practissimo = lots of Viola Time!